The Adventures of Rey the Kitten

Rey

Chippy

Mr. Froggy

DAN LEPPOLD

Illustrations by Mara Chailertphetdee

Fulton Books, Inc.
Meadville, PA

Published by Fulton Books 2021

Edited by Kim Leppold and Jackie Perry

ISBN 978-1-63985-049-5 (paperback)
ISBN 978-1-63985-050-1 (digital)

Printed in the United States of America

For Kim, Rey, Josephine, and Lilly

DWL

1

This is a story about an unlikely friendship. It all started on a spring morning when Rey the Kitten ventured into one of her farm's horse stalls.

3

As Rey walked along the boards of the stall, Sophie the Horse gave out a snort and Rey fell onto the soft hay. Sophie stepped away from Rey, but the kitten was so scared of that big horse hoof she tried to run into a little hole in the boards. Rey was too big and got her head stuck as Sophie the Horse walked out into the pasture.

To Rey's surprise, and to the fright of a chipmunk, she had her head right in the middle of his home! Very scared, the chipmunk let out a loud high-pitched *chip* sound and then another *chip* sound and then another *chip* sound.

Rey said, "Oh, your name must be Chippy. My name is Rey," and she began to purr. Rey explained to Chippy that her head was stuck and that she needed a push.

So Chippy gave her a little push on the nose and out rolled Rey and Chippy.

Rey said, "Thanks, Chippy! Let's be friends."

Chippy said, "But we are not supposed to be friends because everyone says cats chase chipmunks."

Rey said, "Well, that's silly. You are my friend no matter what anyone says."

And with that, a friendship was born. Often, Rey would start her morning by watching the birds eat birdseed on the windowsill. When the time was right, Rey jumped onto the windowsill and made all the birds fly away. Chippy watched all of this, froze, and let out a *chip* sound.

Rey said, "Oh, hi, Chippy. Why don't you fly like the birds do?"

Chippy replied, "I don't have feathers and wings. I have fur like you. I don't fly, but I can run, jump, and climb."

11

Summer

Rey said, "I can run, jump, and climb too. Let's play!"

So Chippy and Rey met outside and jumped in the grass, chased each other, and climbed up into the bushes together.

Summer was arriving and the farm was full of life. Birds were singing, flowers were blooming, and sunshine was all around. As Rey and Chippy played, they heard a strange sound coming from the pond.

"*Ribbet…ribbbbbbet…ribbet.*"

Curious, as most kittens and chipmunks are, they walked together down to the pond to see what was making that odd sound. Little did they know, they were about to make a new friend.

Rey reached out to touch the water and then shook off her wet paw. "I don't like water," Rey said.

Chippy let out a loud *chip* sound as they saw what was making the noise—it was a big frog!

15

The frog felt it was time to introduce himself and said, "Hi! I am Mr. Froggy."

Rey and Chippy told Mr. Froggy that they were scared of the *ribbet* sound. Mr. Froggy said, "Frogs are nothing to be scared of."

They introduced themselves and began to play. Mr. Froggy jumped from lily pad to lily pad as Chippy followed. Rey tried but fell in and quickly swam back to the shore.

And from that day on, Rey, Chippy, and Mr. Froggy were best friends. They played together every day on the farm, jumping and running through the fields of flowers. Once, they even met a friendly bee named Buzzy. The days were becoming shorter, and the nights were becoming cooler. Fall was just around the corner.

19

Fall

One day, Rey the Kitten and Mr. Froggy could not find Chippy. They went into the barn and were surprised to find a note above Chippy's door.

Rey said to Mr. Froggy, "Let's help Chippy."

So Mr. Froggy and Rey set out to collect as many nuts as they could for Chippy. Rey focused on the fields while Mr. Froggy went to the pond where he had noticed some acorns floating near some lily pads.

21

Rey carried walnuts one by one to the edge of the pond while Froggy collected all the floating acorns. They did this for several days until they could find no more nuts. They were very happy with the impressive pile of winter food for their good friend Chippy and were excited to show him.

Rey and Mr. Froggy found Chippy sitting in the jack-o'-lantern, harvesting the last remaining pumpkin seeds. Chippy was delighted to see his friends but, in a sad voice, said, "I am not sure I have enough food for the winter."

That was when Rey and Froggy told Chippy about the pile of nuts they collected for him. And just like that, they saved the day. The three of them carried the nuts to Chippy's home.

25

Winter

As nights drew longer and days became colder, winter arrived. It began to snow. As Rey decorated her tree, she missed her friends, but she knew Mr. Froggy was happy sleeping in the mud under the pond and that Chippy was warm in his home in the barn. Rey the Kitten knew that before long, the snow would melt, the pond would unfreeze, and Chippy would eat his last acorn and have to come out.

Each day, Rey the Kitten would go to the window and look out to see if her friends were back. The days became longer, and the air outside began getting warmer. The snow melted, and the grass began to grow. Each day brought hope and excitement as spring slowly began to wake up from its wintery sleep.

Spring

Spring arrived once again on the farm, and Rey and Chippy were reunited. They jumped and played all the way down to the pond to look for Mr. Froggy. At first, they could not find him, but after looking under some leaves, they heard that nice sound again. *Ribbet, ribbet!* The three friends were back together again.

Throughout the year, Rey the Kitten, Chippy, and Mr. Froggy learned that it doesn't matter how different you are on the outside. All that matters is that you have a loving heart.

The end.

About the Author

Dan Leppold grew up in Pittsburgh, Pennsylvania, became a geologist, and is now a science teacher who teaches high school outside of Philadelphia, Pennsylvania. He lives on a small farm with his wife, Kim, where they raise horses, chickens, and have three cats.

Mara Chailertphetdee owns and operates Lazy Sparrow Studios and was a former student of Mr. Leppold. She is married to Jack Chailertphetdee and enjoys the nature surrounding their home in New Hampshire.

The story of a little kitten named Rey and its unusual friendship with a chipmunk named Chippy and a frog named Froggy is based on true events on a farm outside of Reading, Pennsylvania. Rey was a semiferal kitten that was adopted by Kim and Dan Leppold who remind all of us that we should adopt and not shop for our pets.

CPSIA information can be obtained
at www.ICGtesting.com
Printed in the USA
BVHW020849080322
630901BV00018B/344